AI
MADE
EASY

A Beginner's Guide to Artificial Intelligence

Terri Carbone

ISBN 978-1-63784-789-3 (paperback)
ISBN 978-1-63784-790-9 (digital)

Copyright © 2024 by Terri Carbone

All rights reserved. No part of this publication may be reproduced, distributed, or transmitted in any form or by any means, including photocopying, recording, or other electronic or mechanical methods without the prior written permission of the publisher. For permission requests, solicit the publisher via the address below.

Hawes & Jenkins Publishing
16427 N Scottsdale Road Suite 410
Scottsdale, AZ 85254
www.hawesjenkins.com

Disclaimer: This book is intended for informational purposes only. The technologies and products discussed in this book are mentioned purely for illustrative purposes and do not constitute a recommendation on the author's part. The author has no associations or affiliations with any of the products or corporations discussed here, and her opinions do not necessarily reflect the intentions of those corporations. While the author has made every effort to use reputable sources that reflect the most up-to-date understanding of artificial intelligence as of the writing of this book, AI development is fast-paced. Therefore the author cannot guarantee the accuracy of the content. The author encourages readers to conduct ongoing research and, if necessary or desired, consult relevant professionals for personalized guidance on using AI technologies and products.

Printed in the United States of America

ACKNOWLEDGEMENTS

First and foremost, I give praise to my Heavenly Father and my Lord Jesus Christ for their blessings on this effort.

This book would not have been possible without the amazing collaboration of Sheila Ashdown. You are outstanding in both who you are and in your talent.

Many thanks to my husband, Perry Carbone, for always being supportive of my ideas and my activities.

Special thanks to Julie Campion, Olga Gonzalas, Akshita Thaduri, and Stephen and Amy Smith for your help and perspective. You, with my family, are always there to join with me in taking a positive perspective on the world, seeing what it could be, and helping to make it happen.

INTRODUCTION

So you're curious about artificial intelligence…

"We made your favorite," James said with a smile, setting a heaping plate of chicken parmesan onto the table in front of his sister, Elizabeth. He pulled out his chair and sat down, rounding out the group, which included his wife, Alma, their two kids, and his mom, Lynn. For a moment, the table bustled with activity as everyone passed the dinner rolls and dished out the salad.

"This looks amazing," Elizabeth said, eyes wide. "And it smells amazing, too," she added, taking a deep inhale.

"The kids did most of the work," James said, nodding toward the two teenagers, Madison and Christopher.

"You did?" Elizabeth said. "I'm impressed. When I was your age, the only thing I could cook was boxed mac and cheese."

"Well, we're grateful for the help," Alma, their mother, chimed in. "Work has been so crazy lately; I walked in about two minutes before you got here." She was in good spirits but had exhaustion written on her face and dark circles under her eyes.

"Grandma made the cake, though," Madison said through a mouthful of chicken.

Elizabeth looked at her mom, Lynn. "Is it…?"

"Yep, chocolate with vanilla frosting, just like every year," Lynn assured her. "So be sure to save room."

James said, "So, Elizabeth, it's been a few months since we've seen you. How's work going?"

"Great," she said emphatically. Elizabeth was a journalist and contributed regularly to a tech magazine. "When you write about tech, there's always a new story around the corner, especially with everything going on in AI." The table groaned.

"That artificial intelligence is bad news," Lynn said, shaking her head, eyes wide behind her glasses. "One of my friends from church got a scam phone call from someone using AI. They impersonated her son's voice and tried to scare her into sending money. She said it sounded *just* like him. Lucky for her, her son was with her at the time. But it's scary."

"There's a ton of debate about it at school," said James, who taught high school English. "Some teachers think it's going to rot kids' brains, but there'll always be people who think the worst about new technologies." He shrugged. "I don't personally know a lot about AI, but I'm definitely curious."

"My boss is pressuring me to cut copywriters from my staff and replace them with AI," Alma said. "But I don't think he really knows what he's asking for. He's got dollar signs in his eyes and doesn't seem to care about real people losing their jobs."

"I'm sorry, honey," James said, reaching over to squeeze her hand. "That's gotta be stressful."

They ate in grim silence for a few moments, their fear and anxiety palpable. Elizabeth was used to getting mixed reactions when she told people she wrote about AI, but it hit harder coming from her family, knowing they were being personally affected. She herself was much more optimistic about AI. An enthusiastic early adopter all her life, she found it energizing and exciting to be on the cutting edge.

Trying to tread carefully, Elizabeth said, "AI definitely has its downsides—just like any technology—but, honestly, you're already using AI all day, every day. It's everywhere." She was met by a chorus of disbelief. "I've never used AI," Lynn insisted.

Elizabeth smiled. "Mom, do you watch Netflix?"

"Well, yeah…"

"Then you've used AI."

She then pointed to Christopher's smartphone on the table. "Do you use facial recognition to unlock your phone?"

"Yeah," he said. "It's easy."

"And do you have your voice assistant set up?"

"Siri. She's great!"

"Well, that's AI, too," Elizabeth said. "Along with the Roomba, I see it tucked in the corner over there."

"All of that is artificial intelligence?" her mom asked in disbelief.

"Yep!" Elizabeth said, pleased to see the proverbial lightbulbs turning on for her family.

*****

Like our fictional family, you've undoubtedly heard the phrase: *Artificial Intelligence*. It's all over the news. Your friends, family, and coworkers are buzzing about it. At this point, you're undoubtedly curious, but you may also be feeling confused or anxious. If you are, I don't blame you. The advancements in artificial intelligence are already bringing about huge changes for all of us in every area of our lives, and it's only going to grow. It's normal to have a mix of reactions when faced with a major change, and you're not alone. In a 2023 poll by the Pew Research Center, 52 percent of respondents said they're "more concerned than excited" about the role of AI in daily life.[1]

There are a lot of myths floating around about artificial intelligence, and some of them sound like they're straight out of a science-fiction novel. Myths that AI will eventually gain consciousness, or the ability to feel human emotions, and will perhaps even surpass human intelligence. Myths that machines will take over the world and become a threat to human existence.

But in reality, what we call "artificial intelligence" is just incredibly smart computer programming, done by—you guessed it—humans! And rather than fast-forwarding into a dystopian fictional future, I encourage you to stay closer to the present and focus on the very real ways that these new advances in computer programming are benefiting you right now. It may surprise you to hear this, but you're already immersed in AI. If you stream movies on Netflix, vacuum

---

[1] Michelle Faverio and Alec Tyson, "What the Data Says about Americans' Views of Artificial Intelligence," *Pew Research Center,* November 21, 2023, https://www.pewresearch.org/short-reads/2023/11/21/what-the-data-says-about-americans-views-of-artificial-intelligence/.

your home with a Roomba, use FaceID to open your smartphone, or ask Alexa to play your favorite song, you're using AI. Even though it feels like AI has just arrived, the fact is that it's already ubiquitous. Each one of us is being pulled along on this new AI adventure, and there's no ignoring or avoiding it.

As someone who has had a long career in the technology industry, I've helped a lot of people adapt to new advancements over the years. I've worked as a programmer and project manager, and I've led technical teams at the director level. In 2019, I completed an MIT certificate in Artificial Intelligence: Implications for Business Strategy and began my journey as an AI strategist and transformation guide for companies. My goal is to help individuals and organizations understand how they can benefit from and successfully adopt AI. My philosophy is that AI is a tool, just like the internet is a tool, and it can be used for good or for evil. But if you get proficient with AI, you can use it to bring great benefits to many people.

Increasing my knowledge in the realm of AI is a personal passion of mine, but it's equally important to me to share the wealth and help others understand it too. That being said, this book isn't for everyone. It's not for highly technical people, AI engineers, or enthusiastic early adopters. Rather, it's for those of us who aren't sure if or how AI is going to affect our day-to-day existence. It's for those of us who might feel hesitant or even a bit fearful.

Since AI is such a broad topic, I've tried to make it bite-sized and accessible by focusing on two domains—home life and work life—and telling the story of AI through the lens of a family. Though our family is fictional, they're here to help us see AI through the lens of real-life scenarios that affect the kinds of people you know parents, teachers, and students; healthcare professionals and patients; workers; people of faith; artists; and senior citizens. I empathize with every one of these archetypes. As a mother, I want to help parents keep their kids safe and gain every advantage they can. As a worker, I share the desire to safeguard my job and find new avenues to excel. As a senior, I want to help older people enjoy greater confidence with technology. As a person of faith, I want to help my fellow believers deepen their spiritual practice. As a cancer survivor, I care deeply about the capacity of AI to lead to advancements and cures. As someone with a busy life, I want to help people harness the power of AI to free up time to do more of what they love. I personally empathize with every archetype in this book, so I can speak to your wants, needs, and concerns.

My goal with *AI Made Easy* is to help you gain confidence going forward with the new reality of artificial intelligence. While the specific tools I discuss here will evolve or be replaced in pretty short order, the concepts are long-lasting. In reading this book, you'll build a foundation of understanding that will help you think critically about these powerful new tools and make smart decisions so that you can gain the benefits and avoid the pitfalls.

CHAPTER 1

Building on What You Already Know About AI

"Do you guys remember when you first started using the internet?" Elizabeth asked.

Alma and James looked at each other and laughed. "AOL chat rooms!" They said.

"*You've got mail*," James intoned, mimicking the iconic voice.

"It was back in the nineties. We were in high school," Alma said. "I remember getting those AOL CDs in the mail."

"You had to pay by the minute to use the internet back then," James told his kids.

"What? No way," Christopher said, his face a look of horror.

"I stayed off the internet for as long as I could," Lynn said stoutly. "But then you two were born," she said, gesturing toward her grandkids, "and my friends kept bugging me to share pictures on Facebook."

"And, of course, the kids are digital natives," Alma said. "As a mom, that was challenging for me, trying to figure out how much screen time to allow and how to keep them safe."

"Well, here's something to think about," Elizabeth said. "When we first started using the internet, we were all kind of fumbling around, figuring it out with almost zero guidance. We couldn't have imagined how much it would revolutionize our lives—for better and worse. But could you imagine life without the internet now?" Even Grandma Lynn had to shake her head.

"Wi-fi is life," Madison said.

That got a laugh from the table.

"Pretty soon, you're going to be thinking the same exact thing about AI. You won't know how you ever lived without it. But the difference now is that we're all *so much more tech-savvy* than we were back when the internet became a thing. And there are so many resources out there—books, articles, videos—from smart, helpful people who are sharing their knowledge." "Like you, Aunt Elizabeth," Christopher said.

"Aww! Thanks, bud. That's sweet of you." She looked around the table. She had her family's attention. "Can I tell you about some of the AI technologies out there? I swear, I'll make it painless."

*****

It may seem as if AI has splashed onto the cultural and technological scene all at once, but it's actually been evolving since the 1950s. It's a multifaceted and complex subject, but given that our goal is "AI Made Easy," I'll give just a brief overview to help you get situated, along with examples of some common forms of AI that are already out there. Whether or not you consider yourself tech-savvy, it's valuable to understand the basics of the capabilities and functions of AI, so I encourage you to stay with me as we dig into some technical details.

What is AI?

"Artificial intelligence" is a catch-all term for a broad field of study and a variety of technologies, but the common thread between them is that they're machines programmed to mimic human traits. Depending on the exact nature of the AI, it may be able to move, see, sense, listen, comprehend, analyze, and make decisions.

In the introduction, I mentioned a few well-known examples of AI that you're undoubtedly already familiar with: Netflix, Roomba, voice assistants, and your smartphone's facial unlocking. I'll talk about how AI technologies are working behind the proverbial curtain here.

Netflix's Recommendations Systems

If you shop on Amazon, watch videos on YouTube, or use a streaming service like Netflix or Spotify to watch shows or listen to music, you've no doubt noticed these platforms' uncanny ability to make recommendations tailored to your tastes. That's because these online services employ an AI-powered recommendation system driven by algorithms and machine learning.

This is where a little bit of technical understanding will really go a long way, so stick with me.

Algorithms are used in complex programming, but at their core, algorithms are just a set of rules or processes that a system follows. The basic recipe is that data goes into a system, is processed through a set of rules, and then a result comes out the other side. Using Netflix as an example, the data that goes into the algorithm is… your viewing history (what you watched and for how long), your rating (thumbs up or thumbs down), and information about those titles (name, genre, actors, etc.). The algorithm's purpose is to analyze that data and use it to offer up similar titles.

Netflix also uses a process called *collaborative filtering* to crowd-source recommendations. What happens here is that Netflix has profiles of all of its users, and some of those users share your tastes. So if you and I have a similar profile and you watch and like a particular movie or series, Netflix may recommend it to me too.

Machine learning is the ongoing process by which the algorithm becomes more and more educated about your particular tastes. When you signed up for your Netflix account, you were probably asked to identify a few of your favorite movies or shows. This helped "train" the algorithm. If you named three comedies, Netflix prioritized comedies the next time you logged in. However, humans are complex creatures. You're not a comedy-watching machine, after all. You might be in the mood for something different. You might have a friend over, and they're big into superhero movies. Or your tastes may change over time. Netflix is constantly evolving its inner workings so that the algorithm keeps up with what's current for you.[2]

Roomba's AI Robotics

When it comes to AI, people make a lot of dark jokes about how "our robot overlords" will rule the planet one day. Of course, a lot of us use humor to cope with our discomfort about change, but the truth behind the joke is that it's exactly those kinds of consequences—unwanted and unintended—that make us hesitant to get too cozy with AI. So to get a handle on what's really happening with AI robotics, I figure we should take a look at everybody's favorite robot: Roomba.

If you're uninitiated, Roomba is a small vacuum cleaner that automatically travels through your house, picking up dirt. And in a way, it's a perfect intro to AI for a lot of people, because even if folks are uncertain about AI, we can almost all agree that we hate housework. When Pew Research Center polled Americans in 2022, 57 percent said they're excited by the prospect of using AI for routine household chores.[3]

So how does Roomba work? It uses a combination of robotics, sensors, and AI algorithms, and I'm going to give a quick definition of each.

As you likely already know, *robots* are physical machines, and they're designed to perform tasks.

---

[2] "How Netflix's Recommendations Systems Work," *Netflix*, accessed March 6, 2024, https://help.netflix.com/en/node/100639.

[3] Lee Rainie, Cary Funk, Monica Anderson, and Alec Tyson, "How Americans Think about AI," *Pew Research Center*, March 17, 2022, https://www.pewresearch.org/internet/2022/03/17/how-americans-think-about-artificial-intelligence/.

Sensors are instruments that detect things in our physical environment. There's a big variety of sensors, and they are *everywhere*. At the grocery store, when the automatic sliding doors open, it may be a pressure-sensitive weight sensor that "feels" you standing on top of it. If you've got motion-activated lights in your yard, those work by flipping on a light when the sensor "sees" someone move. If your car helps you steer clear of collisions when you're parking, it's using a sensor system that emits soundwaves and then measures how long it takes for those soundwaves to bounce back. This is how it judges distance and can helpfully beep at you before you do any bumping.[4] In the case of Roomba, sensors are what give it its sense of perception, so it can avoid running into your furniture or falling down the stairs.

Roomba takes things to the next level by adding *AI algorithms* to the mix. (Remember, an algorithm is a set of rules that a system follows.) iRobot (the maker of Roomba) calls it the "Dirt Detective." It's got multiple functions, but one thing the Dirt Detective does is determine which areas of your home are the dirtiest. It likely takes more time and a greater number of passes to clean the floor in your kitchen or around the litter box than, say, your guest bedroom. So Roomba collects that data and refers back to it the next time it goes out to clean, and it cleans those dirtier areas first.[5] That's machine learning—similar to what we just saw with Netflix—when the machine uses data it collected in the past to make predictions about the future.

Alexa, Siri, and AI Language Processing

AI voice assistants like Alexa and Siri have practically become members of the family these days, haven't they? They're especially helpful when you've got your hands full. Maybe you're washing dishes, and you ask your voice assistant to put on some music because

---

[4] "Parking Sensors," *National Safety Commission*, accessed March 11, 2024, https://mycardoeswhat.org/safety-features/parking-sensors/.

[5] "iRobot OS," *iRobot*, accessed March 11, 2024, https://www.irobot.com/en US/irobot-os.html.

you're elbow-deep in suds. Or you're driving and need some directions. You can use these AI-powered helpers to give you a reminder, set a timer, schedule an event, search the internet, call a friend, and so much more.

Now, there's a ton of variation in the way people speak. Language, accent, speed, slang, sarcasm, idiomatic expressions, and so on. Given all that, it won't surprise you to hear that the technology that goes into making these voice assistants is quite complex. However, for our purposes, we don't need to get into the nitty-gritty. We'll just take a high-level look at some of the most important aspects.

Let's say, for example, you've got a friend named Carl, and you want to give him a call. You might say, "Hey, Siri, call Carl." What happens next?

When you call out "Hey, Siri," that's called the *wake word*. Makes sense, right? You're effectively "waking up" your voice assistant and priming it to get ready for your question or request.

Now that your voice assistant is awake, it uses a type of algorithm called *automatic speech recognition* to turn your voice into text so that it can be read by the computer. It does this by capturing the audio ("Call Carl"), filtering out any background noise, and then breaking the audio down into the most basic parts of spoken language: phonemes. On average, a language has twenty to sixty phonemes.[6] You can think of a phoneme like an atom. Just like atoms are the smallest unit of physical matter, phonemes are the smallest unit of speech.

Your computer then uses *language modeling* algorithms to predict how those phonemes should most likely be put together to form words and sentences. Language models are based on patterns and statistics, such as common sentence structures and the most frequently used words. (Have you used the "predictive text" feature on your smartphone? If so, you've definitely seen language modeling in

---

[6] Preethi Jyothi, "Automatic Speech Recognition: An Overview," *Microsoft Research* YouTube channel, September 11, 2017, YouTube video, https://youtu.be/q67z7PTGRi8?si=baA5XOX1Nwprz3u2.

action. It's what allows your phone to suggest the next word in the sentence while you're typing it.)

Once your computer has accurately transcribed your words, it uses *natural language processing* to *understand* what you're saying so that it can take action on it. It identifies the parts of speech (nouns, verbs, adjectives, etc.) so that it can create a logical sentence structure. It identifies proper nouns (for example, it identifies "Carl" as a person's name). And it recognizes your intent—in this case, the intent is a command: "Call Carl."[7]

Next step: *query processing*. In short, the system figures out what it needs to do to give you what you asked for. In this case, it has to open your telephone, access your contacts, and call Carl. And finally, it generates a response by using *text-to-speech* to verbally tell you what it's doing. It'll say to you something like, "Calling Carl."

I know that's a lot. And to think this all happens within the span of just a few seconds, it's pretty mind-boggling.

And, just to put a cherry on top of this topic, I want to point out that these voice assistants get better and better at their jobs through *machine learning*. You've heard this phrase before in the sections on both Netflix and Roomba, and I'm repeating it here because machine learning is such an important component of artificial intelligence. The more we, as humans, speak to our voice assistants, the more data we provide as to how real people actually talk. With more of that data to pull from, voice assistants will get more accurate in their ability to hear, understand, and talk.

Smartphones and Facial Recognition

Facial recognition software is another AI advancement that's so commonplace, you might have forgotten it's AI. For a lot of us, it's become second nature to unlock our smartphones just by looking

---

[7] "What Is Natural Language Processing (NLP)?" *IBM*, accessed March 18, 2024, https://www.ibm.com/topics/natural-language-processing.

at them. This is done using two types of technologies we've already discussed: sensors and AI algorithms.

In the case of your smartphone, the *sensor* is, of course, the camera, which gives the computer the ability to see you. However, in the case of facial recognition, this camera is taking a different type of photo than you're used to. Unlike a typical two-dimensional photo, these special 3D cameras also capture *depth* and *heat*. It creates a "depth map" that captures the unique contours of your features—something like a topographical map—as well as the patterns of heat across your face.[8] Together, these create the unique signature of your face.

Once you "enroll" in facial recognition and you take the initial 3D photo, that's the photo that's referenced every time you unlock your phone.

So then the next big question is: How does your phone match you—the you that has just picked up your phone—with the original reference photo?

Well, buckle up, because this is another big deal in AI, and it's called an *artificial neural network*. Stay with me; we're going to make this painless, okay?

As you know, we have a neural network in our human brain, and one of its functions is to make decisions. Artificial neural networks are designed to mimic this process. Just like you, it makes decisions by processing all of the variables and giving an appropriate weight to each one.[9] In real life, let's say you're trying to decide whether or not to go to a party. It's Friday evening, and you're tired and grumpy from a long workweek, and you've looked in the closet and have nothing to wear. Based on those variables, you're in no mood for a party. However, the party is for your best friend's birthday. So you assign a "weight" to each of these variables, and in all likelihood, the fact that it's your best friend's birthday heavily outweighs the fact

---

[8] "About Face ID Advanced Technology," *Apple,* January 10, 2024, https://support.apple.com/en-us/102381.

[9] Martin Keen, "Neural Networks Explained in Five Minutes," *IBM Technology* YouTube channel, May 24, 2022, YouTube video, https://www.youtube.com/watch?v=jmmW0F0biz0.

that you're tired, grumpy, and have nothing to wear. So you go to the party (and hopefully have a good time).

Just like you, artificial neural networks "do the math"—only, while you do it figuratively, they do it literally.

In the case of facial recognition, the decision-making is done with a special type of neural network called a *convolutional neural network*. ("Convolutional" is a mathematics term, but we're going to skip the numbers and stick to the concepts.) The important thing to know is that this neural network is specifically related to computer vision, and it allows your smartphone to apply that weighted decision-making process to an image. It works by first breaking out the image into its smallest units, which are pixels. It then analyzes the pixels by overlaying a series of filters, with the goal of identifying relevant patterns and features. If a pixel (or group of pixels) is deemed relevant to your original reference photo, it's assigned a higher weight than a pixel that is less relevant. This process is rinsed and repeated, sometimes tens or hundreds of times. And once the process is complete and the most relevant pixels are identified, the program determines that there's a high probability that *you* are, in fact, *you*.[10][11] And voilà, your phone unlocks. All in an instant.

* * * * *

"Uh, Aunt Elizabeth, no offense, but that was a lot," Madison chimed in.

"I know," Elizabeth said, hands up in surrender. "I swear, I'm not trying to melt your minds."

"There's too much to remember!"

"Well," Elizabeth countered. "You just learned a lot of the really foundational stuff." She counted it off on her fingers. "We talked

---

[10] Alexander Amini, "MIT 6.S191: Convolutional Neural Networks," *Alexander Amini* YouTube channel, March 24, 2023, YouTube video, https://youtu.be/NmLK_WQBxB4?si=ftUK-O5qoF7CDQkD.

[11] Lev Craig and Rahul Awati, "What Is a Convolutional Neural Network (CNN)?," *TechTarget*, updated January 2024, https://www.techtarget.com/searchenterpriseai/definition/convolutional-neural-network.

about recommendation systems—those are everywhere. Not just Netflix, but Amazon, Spotify, et cetera. We also talked about sensors, language modeling, and neural networks. And we talked about machine learning—"

"That's how the algorithm gets better, yeah?" Madison interrupted, her eyes bright.

"Exactly!" Elizabeth was pumped to see her niece getting excited. "Do you remember how?"

Madison thought for a second. "Well, if the algorithm uses data to make a prediction, then the more data it has, the better chance it'll make a good prediction."

"Yes! You're getting it."

"It certainly seems less scary the way you describe it," Lynn added, seeming relieved.

"I'm glad to hear that." Elizabeth hated to think of her mom—or anybody—as being scared of technology. "Do you guys want to hear more? I could talk about this stuff all day."

"Okay!"

"Awesome! Let's talk about some of the ways we can use AI in our day-to-day lives at home."

CHAPTER 2

AI at Home

As our friend Elizabeth has shown, AI is all around us. But in this chapter, we're going to turn our attention to the AI technologies that we can use in our homes, families, and private lives. One thing you'll notice is how much of what we touch on in this chapter builds on what we explored in the previous chapter. That's because, even though AI is a broad field, product developers are always looking for ways to use existing technologies in novel ways. So you'll start to think, "Oh, I've seen that before!" Hopefully, you're already starting to feel the sense of empowerment that comes with building a basic understanding of AI. When used wisely, AI can help us get more of what we want out of life and less of what we don't, but the only way to use it wisely—and fearlessly—is from a well-informed place.

Globally, we're in an interesting spot with our digital development. There are plenty of us who remember life before the internet, and there are also plenty of digital natives who've never known life without it. Our fictional family spans the gamut. I'm sure you know younger folks like our teenagers Madison and Christopher, for whom wi-fi is life; Gen Xers like James and Alma, who are tech savvy but also probably grateful there's no digital evidence of their youthful antics; and Grandma Lynn, who reluctantly joined social media once she could no longer resist the temptation to share photos of her grandkids.

Since the internet has become a staple of our lives, the persistent connection to the outside world has been a blessing and a curse. At the outset, we didn't know what we were getting ourselves into: the incredible opportunities, yes, but also the dark web, hackers, scammers, predators, and whole industries that have cropped up to mine and sell our private data. In this chapter, we'll explore some of the opportunities available, but we'll also talk about some of the downsides—and how to avoid them.

And just to reiterate, the goal of *AI Made Easy* is to cultivate your mindset and your thinking around AI. We'll use specific technologies for demonstration purposes, but I can almost guarantee a new technology will have launched by the time I finish writing this chapter.

AI Webchats: Your Personal Research Assistant

You've already met Alma and James, a couple of full-time working parents with two teenage kids. If you've ever been in their shoes, you know what a herculean effort it can be to balance it all. In fact, in a 2018 survey by the Pew Research Center, 74 percent of parents of kids under 18 reported being *too busy to enjoy life* at least some of the time.[12] I'm sure Alma and James feel that way sometimes, and maybe you do too.

The general awareness of AI really skyrocketed in 2022 with the release of OpenAI's ChatGPT, an online webchat that generates a human-like text in response to a question or request. ChatGPT may be the most well-known AI webchat at the time of writing, but there are others on the market, such as Microsoft's Copilot (which was developed in partnership with ChatGPT) and Google's Gemini. AI webchat technology is worth knowing about because it's wide-reaching and useful.

In the introduction, we talked about voice assistants like Siri and Alexa and how they use natural language processing to under-

---

[12] Patrick Van Kessel, "How Americans Feel about the Satisfactions and Stresses of Modern Life," *Pew Research Center*, February 5, 2020, https://www.pewresearch.org/short-reads/2020/02/05/how-americans-feel-about-the-satisfactions-and-str esses-of-modern-life/.

stand and respond to your voice. AI webchats use that same technology, only with written language as opposed to spoken.

A big differentiator, though, between voice assistants and AI webchats is that webchats use a type of AI called *generative AI*. In generative AI, the program creates *new* content based on what it's learned from *existing* content,[13] and that existing content is what's called *training data*. Here's an easy way to understand this: What's a subject you're passionate about or knowledgeable about? If you and I were to meet and I asked you a question about the subject, you'd undoubtedly draw on what you already know in order to answer my question. Everything you learned in the past is like the training data, and it's what allows you to come up with a novel answer that fits the present context of our conversation. That's how AI webchats work: only the training data is text pulled from all over the internet—including blogs, websites, books, and social media—and the webchat's algorithms analyze that data to find patterns in it. Understanding those patterns allows the algorithm to predict what kind of response makes sense given the context.[14]

In your daily life, generative AI webchats can serve as your on-call research assistant. Let's say Alma and James are meal-planning for the week. They just went to Costco and stocked up on chicken, but are feeling uninspired as far as to what to do with it. So they go to an AI webchat.

"Please recommend five chicken recipes," Alma types.

They like what they see, but then James says, "We should ask it for chicken recipes that can be made in under twenty minutes. We've got a really busy week coming up, and we're not going to want to spend a bunch of time cooking."

So, Alma types in a new query: "Please recommend five chicken recipes that can be made in under twenty minutes."

---

[13] Gwendolyn Stripling, "Introduction to Generative AI," *Google Cloud Tech* YouTube channel, May 8, 2023, YouTube video, https://www.youtube.com/watch?v=G2fqAlgmoPo.

[14] Shreya Johri, "The Making of ChatGPT: From Data to Dialogue," *Science in the News* blog, Harvard University, June 6, 2023, https://sitn.hms.harvard.edu/flash/2023/the-making-of-chatgpt-from-data-to-dialogue/.

What Alma did just then is called *prompt engineering*, which is just a high-tech way of saying she tweaked her request to get a more relevant answer. Generative AI has one goal: to give you what you ask for. And so if you don't quite get what you want the first time around, you simply revise your request until you're satisfied.

And so, Alma and James have five chicken recipes, and they also had the webchat make the grocery list too!

Of course, meal planning is just one of the ways you can use webchats for help in your day-to-day life. You can use it any time you need a virtual research assistant to help with planning or inspiration: plan a party or holiday gathering, get new inspiration for a date night with your spouse, or ask it to recommend games to play with your kids or grandkids.

AI for a Safer, More Efficient Home

For homeowners, two of the greatest promises of AI are *safety* and *efficiency*. There's a wide range of "smart" home devices on the market—with more coming all the time—that can help you upgrade on both scores.

Our fictional family has five members under one roof. Between packages, food delivery, and all sorts of friends and family (they're social butterflies who love to entertain), traffic at their front door rivals Grand Central Station. They're exactly the kind of people who would benefit from a smart doorbell to help them manage it all.

Smart doorbells, such as Ring, are popular options at the moment, and it may surprise you to hear they're AI-powered. Smart doorbells use *sensors* (in this case, a camera and microphone) and AI *image recognition* technology. When something comes into view of your doorbell's camera, the algorithm classifies the object and alerts you when it sees something relevant. In this case, of course, it's usually people and packages.

In the book's introduction, we talked about unlocking your smartphone using facial authentication, so you've already got a basic handle on how AI recognizes images. So here's what makes these two technologies similar: in the case of both smart doorbells and facial authentication, the computer is comparing a *new* image against a set of *stored images* in order to make a match.

But here's where these two technologies differ: when you pick up your smartphone and show it your face, it only compares this new image with the stored images you enrolled during setup. But with a smart doorbell, it compares every new image against a much broader set of stored images, which is the training data. To refresh your memory, training data is preexisting data that's already been fed into the algorithm. In the case of webchats, the training data is text. In the case of a smart doorbell, the training data is images. So before you ever bought your smart doorbell, its algorithm was fed hundreds or thousands of images of, for example, packages being delivered to doors. Referring to its training data, the algorithm uses pattern recognition to determine whether the object in view is a squirrel, a bird, or a FedEx driver dropping off your latest sweet find from eBay.

From an efficiency standpoint, there are a slew of smart home products on the market that customize and control the energy usage in your home, increasing your comfort while potentially saving you money. One example is AI-powered smart thermostats like Nest, which use *temperature sensors* and *AI algorithms*. As you'll recall, sensors are devices that detect aspects of our physical environment. In the case of Nest, the sensors allow the system to detect the temperature in the room, and then the algorithm helps the system decide what to do with that information.

For example, let's say you have one sensor in your home office and one in your bedroom, and you like to stay warm during the day but cooler at night. You can set Nest to prioritize the home office sensor during the daytime and your bedroom sensor at night.[15] That way, the system heats or cools according to your preferences without you having to fiddle with the thermostat or wake up in a sweat because you forgot to turn the temperature down before bed. Nest

---

[15] "Learn about the Nest Temperature Sensor," *Google*, accessed March 21, 2024, https://support.google.com/googlenest/answer/9248154?sjid=2220988310 384319921-NC.

can even monitor your HVAC system and alert you when maintenance is needed. For example, if Nest notices your home takes longer than usual to heat up or cool down, it'll send you an alert.[16]

These are just two examples of the types of AI-powered products out there that can help smarten up your home. There are smart bulbs, smart locks, smart blinds, smart appliances, and more. What are your personal concerns for your home? I bet there's an AI-powered solution worth checking out.

AI for Safer, Happier Kids

We all know the internet is a mixed bag of the good and the bad, and as tech-savvy adults, we've developed strategies for gaining the benefits while (hopefully) avoiding the downsides. Our children crave digital access. You can probably imagine our teenagers, Christopher and Madison, relentlessly begging their parents for smartphones and permission to use the hottest social media du jour. And Alma and James, their older and wiser parents, weigh the pros and cons. With two extroverted kids and their schedules jam-packed with friends, sports, and after-school activities, they can see how smartphones will help them stay connected and organized. But they also know it's up to them as parents to help their kids develop their internet street smarts and protect them along the way.

Fortunately, digital child-safety measures have evolved to support parents' efforts, and AI is helping. One way is through content monitoring, which can be done with apps like Bark. Bark can be installed on any internet-connected device, and it uses AI to monitor online content like texts, emails, websites, and social media. If Bark detects any issues—bullying, violence, or predatory behavior—the parent receives an alert. While Bark doesn't give exact details on how it accomplishes this (technology companies often don't want to

---

[16] "HVAC monitoring from Google Nest," *Google*, accessed March 21, 2024. https://support.google.com/googlenest/answer/9984225?p=hvac_monitoring&visit_id=637395180762856947-1213971903&rd=1.

reveal what's in their "secret sauce"), we can assume Bark is using a *large language model* to do *contextual analysis*.

We touched on language modeling in the section on AI voice assistants, so you already know that language models are designed to use patterns and statistics to understand sentence structure and the meaning of the words within the sentence.

But as we all know, words have different meanings based on their context, and these distinctions can be critical. Bark uses this chilling example to show the difference: "If you're late to chemistry again, Ms. Jones will kill you" versus "I'm scared Tyler will bring a gun to school and kill someone."[17] The first is an obvious hyperbole, while the second is genuinely alarming. To understand the difference, Bark likely uses contextual analysis to "understand the context of each word in a sentence by considering it in relation to every other word" (Martin Keen, IBM).[18]

When it comes to online content monitoring, it's the *context*, not just the particular words, that reign supreme. With effective contextual analysis, there's a greater chance the system will flag the most relevant content, which means you're less likely to miss something important and also less likely to be flooded with irrelevant alerts. "Alert fatigue" is a genuine phenomenon. If you get a lot of false positives, they start to become noise, and you're more likely to miss something important.

Of course, when you do receive an alert, the most important part is *what you do with it*. In an ideal scenario, an alert is a conversation starter that gives you the opportunity to connect with your kid and learn more about what's going on in their world and how you can help or support them. There's no substitute for an honest, authentic connection between humans, and AI can be an amazing tool to facilitate that.

---

[17] Haley Zapal, "Everything You Need to Know about Bark's Content Monitoring," Bark blog, November 20, 2023, https://www.bark.us/blog/advanced-content-monitoring/.

[18] Martin Keen, "How Large Language Models Work," *IBM Technology* YouTube channel, July 28, 2023, YouTube video, https://youtu.be/5sLYAQS9sWQ?si=bRWAxAobNPalqCb8.

AI for Your Personal Health and Well-Being

"Hey," Elizabeth said to James, pointing at her brother's wrist. "You're wearing a smartwatch." "I am," he said.

"You know that's chock-full of AI, right?"

Elizabeth could practically see the light bulb go on over his head.

"Duh," he said, smacking himself lightly on the forehead. "I honestly didn't even think about it." "That's okay. There's not room in the family for *two* genius siblings," she cracked.

James rolled his eyes good-naturedly. "I guess it does go to show how much AI we're already using every day," he said. "I like to check out the stats on my biometrics."

Grandma Lynn broke in. "What are biometrics?"

"It depends on the smartwatch, but biometrics can include things like your heart rate, the number of steps you take, or how long you sleep."

"Your watch can tell you all that?"

* * * * *

For centuries, people have been creating systems to track their health habits. Leonardo da Vinci is thought to be the first inventor of a mechanical pedometer, and Benjamin Franklin tracked his daily habits in accordance with the thirteen virtues he outlined for himself. In modern times, of course, we have more high-tech ways of monitoring our health. There's a huge market for wearable devices that can monitor physical activity, heart rate, blood pressure, sleep quality, and more.

Considering that more than twelve percent of Americans use a smartwatch[19], if you don't own one yourself, you likely know someone who does. The market for these popular devices is expected to

---

[19] Rohit Shewale, "Smartwatch Statistics 2024: Worldwide Market Data," Demand Sage, March 24, 2024, https://www.demandsage.com/smartwatch-statistics/.

grow, and you may want to take advantage of their built-in AI capabilities that can help you track important health metrics.

One potentially lifesaving feature is heart rate monitoring. Smartwatches monitor your heart rate on your wrist, and some newer models can even alert you if or when something unusual occurs, like an irregular heartbeat.

How does it work? First, let's back up for a second. As you know, when you take your pulse, you typically place your fingers at your neck or wrist. You feel that familiar "bump" as blood pulses, then a pause, and then another bump (and so on). What you're feeling here is the increase and decrease of blood volume as your heart beats. There is more volume at the bump and less volume during the pause.

Smartwatches measure that blood volume by using an *optical sensor*. This may sound a little wild, but stay with me. Optical sensors measure light, and the way they work in this context can be explained by the science of color. The reason blood appears red to the human eye is because blood reflects red light and absorbs green light. So the smartwatch flashes green LED light hundreds of times per second at your wrist, and it measures *when* the green light is absorbed and *how much* is absorbed. Anytime your pulse beats, there's a higher volume of blood at that moment, and so a higher amount of green light is absorbed. By calculating the green-light absorption, the watch can determine your heart rate (the number of times your heart beats per minute).[20] You can look at that info to see your heart rate when you're at rest and during various physical activities.

Some newer smartwatches even go a step further, using *electrocardiogram (ECG) sensors* to measure your heart's electrical signals, which produces "a photograph of how electricity is moving through the heart" (Roger Seheult, MD). ECGs are used to diagnose common heart issues like atrial fibrillation (rapid or irregular heartbeat), which can indicate a risk of stroke.[21]

---

[20] "Monitor Your Heart Rate with Apple Watch," Apple, September 21, 2023, https://support.apple.com/en-us/HT204666#sensors.

[21] Roger Seheult, "ECG Watch: How It Works (Apple, Samsung Afib Watches/EKG)," *Med Cram: Medical Lectures Explained* YouTube channel, December 8, 2021, YouTube video, https://youtu.be/0HxOWCw4hEU?si=19nqLirEqcrfoWNM.

While it's the sensors that gather the raw data, it's the *AI algorithms* that allow the device (and you) to make meaning from that information. Heart data gives insight into your stress levels and emotional well-being and can help you track data from potentially irregular heart events. All this information you gather from your smartwatch can be a talking point with your doctor and can be a catalyst for helping you make heart-healthy decisions in your lifestyle and medical regimens.

AI for Independent Senior Living

"What do you think, Mom? Should we get you a smartwatch for Christmas this year?"

Grandma Lynn raised an eyebrow, a dubious look on her face. "I go to my doctor regularly. I'm not sure I need that around-the-clock monitoring."

"Well," Elizabeth countered. "That may be true, but have any of your friends had a bad fall?"

Lynn blanched. "Oh my, *yes*. One of my friends fell down the basement stairs on her way to do laundry. Her daughter found her three hours later because she couldn't get her on the phone and started to worry."

"Mom, you didn't tell us about that," James scolded.

Lynn seemed sheepish. "I didn't want you to worry that the same thing could happen to me."

*****

Everyone wants to age well and remain healthy and independent for as long as possible, and there are AI products across many industries that can support these goals. Wearables, like smartwatches, are just the tip of the iceberg. There are brain-training apps that can support cognitive health; there are AI-enhanced pill dispensers (some with facial recognition for security); and some retirement communities even have self-driving cars to shuttle residents around the grounds. As we'll touch on later, the use of AI in medical imaging, surgery, and pharmaceutical development has contributed to longevity by allowing for faster, more accurate diagnosis and treatment of disease and illness.

One important AI technology to know about is fall detection. Falls are the number two cause of death worldwide, according to the World Health Organization, and people sixty years and older suffer the most falls.[22] What happened to Lynn's friend is sadly common, and falls can have tragic consequences, including hospitalization, long-term disability, or death.

After that grim news, you'll be relieved to hear that AI technology is here to help. Fall-detection technology has come a long way since the days of "I've fallen and I can't get up!" And it doesn't have to come in the form of a clunky-looking medical device. Nowadays, everyday wearables like watches, pendants, and rings are built with the ability to use *sensors* and *AI algorithms* to detect a fall and call for medical attention. While there are different systems out there, the sensors may include an *accelerometer*, which can detect sudden movement, and a *gyroscope*, which can detect a sudden change in angle or rotation. So if you were to, say, trip down a set of stairs or roll out of bed, the sensors would capture the data, and the AI algorithm would be able to assess that data and determine that it matches the movement pattern of a sudden fall.

You certainly don't need to buy all the latest and greatest gadgets (unless you want to, of course), but if you're too wary about AI to learn how it can benefit you, you may miss out on opportunities for peace of mind.

AI to Deepen Your Religious Practice

So far, we've talked about how AI can save you time and money and contribute to the health and safety of you and your loved ones.

---

[22] "Falls," World Health Organization, April 26, 2021, https://www.who.int/news-room/fact-sheets/detail/falls.

All great things, of course. But what we haven't talked about yet is how AI tools can support your passions. If there's something in your life that's deeply meaningful for you, there's likely an AI tool that can help. For me, my Christian faith is my passion. If you share that journey with me, AI tools can help you deepen your relationship with God, better understand your faith, and help you share it with others.

In an earlier section, we talked about using generative AI web chats like Copilot, ChatGPT, or Gemini as virtual research assistants for daily chores, but these tools can also be used to spark inspiration around your faith.

Take Lynn, the matriarch of our family. She's nearly eighty and has never gotten quite comfortable with the internet. She has a smartphone, but only because her son, James, bought it for her. Besides email and a little social media, she doesn't see much use for the internet in her own life. However, Lynn is very active with her church and feels that this is what life is all about: real, in-person connections with people who share her faith.

Lynn teaches Sunday school to elementary-age kids and facilitates a Bible study group for adults, and what she probably doesn't know is how much generative AI could be helping her prepare for both. While the teachings of the Bible are relevant for people at all stages of life, they need to be told in an age-appropriate way. If Lynn is feeling inspired to teach the story of Daniel and the Lion's Den, for example, she could use an AI webchat to find a child-friendly summary of the story along with a fifteen-minute lesson plan and maybe even a fun craft project. In just a few moments, generative AI could provide an interactive, age-appropriate lesson that suits the attention span of young kids. Then, if Lynn wants to lead a session on Daniel and the Lion's Den with her adult Bible study, she could ask the webchat for a list of discussion questions or sermons.

This is just one of the many ways we can use AI tools to facilitate—not replace—the person-to-person connections that enrich our lives so much.

The Downsides to AI in Your Private Life

As with any new technology, it's fair to have anxieties. Most of us remember the birth of the internet and how it grew to eventually become an indispensable part of our lives. AI is the new wave. (I almost wrote "*next* wave," but it's not next—it's already here!) Disruptive technology like this has always brought advancements and opportunities. Think about some of the commonplace technologies—electricity, the printing press, and cars—that were disruptive and controversial in their time. We wouldn't want to go back to life before their existence, and it's only a matter of time before we feel the same about AI.

But as with any tool, there are downsides. AI is already being used and abused by bad actors, and we need to be aware of the risks and pitfalls so we can steer clear of them.

Your Private Data Is Out There

"You know what was weird?" James asked. "The other day, Christopher and I were in the living room talking about this scooter he wants to get, and ever since then, I've been seeing ads for it everywhere. I even got a flier in the mail."

"That happens to me all the time," Alma said. "It makes me feel like I'm under surveillance," she added, annoyed.

"I like it," Christopher said with a laugh. "Anything to convince you guys to buy me new stuff." He craned his head toward the living room and called out in a loud voice, "PlayStation! Great deals on PlayStations!"

"Well, you're not imagining things," Elizabeth said ruefully. "I wish you were. But if you've got your smart TV set up to use voice commands, it's probably using 'active listening' technology, which listens to ambient conversation and picks up on keywords and phrases."

Alma had an appalled look on her face. "And what exactly do they *do* with that information?"

Elizabeth had to shrug. "Your guess is as good as mine, but most likely they sell it."

The unease around the table was palpable, as everyone had good reason to wonder if what they were about to say next was going to be recorded.

"But who cares?" Christopher asked. "I'm not doing anything wrong, so why does it matter?" "Oh, it matters," Elizabeth insisted.

*****

In a 2023 survey of over forty-five thousand American adults, Publishers Clearing House (PCH) Consumers. The Insights group found that 82 percent of respondents consider themselves "private people," and 77 percent say they're cautious about security.[23] If you're like most people, you're concerned about data privacy. And if you're not, you should be.

Unfortunately, we're living in a data-driven economy where our personal information is a valuable commodity. Much of the data collection is done by data brokers, which are companies that collect your personal information, package it into a user profile, and sell it to corporations, governments, and scammers. Legitimate businesses use this information to create detailed consumer profiles, which in turn allow them to create hyper-targeted marketing and advertising campaigns. Depending on our personal philosophy, this may seem either intrusive or helpful.

On the criminal side, scammers buy (or steal) our personal data for all manner of nefarious purposes. According to the nonprofit organization Identity Theft Research Center, 2023 was a record-breaking year for data compromises: 3,205 incidents in the United States, with over 350 million victims. (Yes, more victims than the entire

---

[23] Tiffany Johnson, Daniela Molta, and Evan Shapiro, "It's All Personal: A Study on Consumer Attitude toward Data Collection and Usage," *Publishers Clearing House Consumer Insights*, 2023, https://insights.pch.com/img/data-ethics-design.pdf.

population of the country.)[24] And in 2021, data broker Epsilon was fined $150 million for knowingly selling consumer profiles to companies that were using the information to attempt to defraud elderly people.[25]

If you're shocked, appalled, and wondering why you don't know more about this, you're not alone. PCH Consumer Insights survey found that only 51 percent of people "feel informed about how their personal data is being used by companies, government, and social entities."[26] (And I must point out, just because a person *feels* informed doesn't necessarily mean they truly *are* informed.) The data economy is invisible and mostly unregulated since, in the United States, there are no comprehensive federal laws protecting data privacy, and the average person has no way to view or edit any profile a data broker may have created.[27]

Of course, data brokering, hacking, and scamming are nothing new, but artificial intelligence tools have given bad actors a new set of sophisticated tools, and it's important to stay up-to-date and vigilant so you can protect yourself to the best of your ability. In the next section, we'll talk about some AI-powered scams and how to avoid them.

---

[24] "2023 Data Breach Report," *Identity Theft Resource Center*, January 2024, https://www.idtheftcenter.org/wp-content/uploads/2024/01/ITRC_2023-Annual-Data-Breach-Report.pdf.

[25] US Department of Justice, Office of Public Affairs, "Marketing Company Agrees to Pay $150 Million for Facilitating Elder Fraud Schemes," press release, January 27, 2021, https://www.justice.gov/opa/pr/marketing-company-agrees-pay-150-million-facilitating-elder-fraud-schemes.

[26] Tiffany Johnson, Daniela Molta, and Evan Shapiro, "It's All Personal: A Study on Consumer Attitude toward Data Collection and Usage," *Publishers Clearing House Consumer Insights*, 2023, https://insights.pch.com/img/data-ethics-design.pdf.

[27] "Data Brokers," *Electronic Privacy Information Center*, accessed April 2, 2024, https://epic.org/issues/consumer-privacy/data-brokers/.

TERRI CARBONE

AI-Powered Scams

It's tempting to fall into the mindset of Christopher, the teenage son of the family, who wonders if data privacy matters if he's not "doing anything wrong." That's a common dismissal. But consider a situation I experienced myself:

A while back, I got a FaceTime video call from the pastor at a church I used to attend. I was surprised, since I hadn't been to that church in about five years, but I accepted the call. After we exchanged greetings, my pastor asked me for money. This was an unusual request, and it immediately set off alarm bells for me, so I began asking some probing questions—and, in the background, I could hear a couple of men whispering amongst themselves, trying to figure out how to reply. Because, of course, this wasn't my pastor at all. It was a group of scammers using AI deepfake technology to create plausible video and audio that mimicked the look and voice of my pastor. The jig was up as soon as I started asking questions the scammers couldn't answer.

When word of the scam got back to the pastor, he alerted his church members, but for some people, it was too late; they'd already been tricked into sending money. And while we all like to think we're too savvy to fall for a scam, you never know until you're facing one yourself. In the case of a pastor, he's a trustworthy person who cares about his congregation, and churches *do* request donations. So the premise of the scam was plausible. And some people probably had no idea it was even possible to use technology to create a realistic AI facsimile.

My pastor hadn't done anything wrong. He probably had videos of sermons or other religious content on social media or YouTube, and scammers harvested snippets and used them to perpetrate a scheme. So even though you personally have nothing to hide, it doesn't mean your personal data can't be used in a harmful way.

Scammers prey on us by exploiting what we hold dear. In the case of my pastor, it was a trusting relationship with his congregation. And for a mother in Arizona, it was her love for her daughter. In 2023, Jennifer DeStefano relayed this story to the US Senate: she picked up a phone call, and on the other end was her fifteen-year-old daughter, terrified and sobbing for help, crying, "Bad men have me." Then, kidnappers came on the line to demand ransom, or else they were going to kill her daughter. As you can imagine, absolute terror and pandemonium ensued as DeStefano leapt into action to get help and negotiate a ransom amount. They settled on $50,000 and demanded that DeStefano herself be kidnapped and taken to an unknown location to hand over the money. She was prepared to go through with it.

Fortunately, as DeStefano was negotiating with her daughter's kidnappers, someone was able to reach DeStefano's husband. Her husband was able to confirm that their daughter was home and safe in bed. Not kidnapped. Not in any danger at all.

After what was the most harrowing experience of her life, one that has left her traumatized, DeStefano was told she had absolutely no legal recourse. The police chalked it up to a "prank" call. It was cruel and intended to harm, but since no one had been kidnapped and no money had been exchanged, technically, no crime had been committed. And so DeStefano was on her own to deal with the fear, paranoia, and post-traumatic stress caused by this attack.[28]

Even though stories like this are scary, I share them because knowledge is power. If you're aware of just how convincing these AI-powered scams can be, you're more likely to be able to stop and assess the situation if it happens to you. You can safeguard against this particular type of scam by coming up with a verbal safe word only known to you and your family. That way, if you're ever faced with a situation like the DeStefanos, you can ask for the verbal safe word, and if the person on the other end of the line can't provide it, they're *not* your loved one. Hang up.

*****

---

[28] US Senate Judiciary Subcommittee on Human Rights and the Law, Hearing on Artificial Intelligence and Human Rights, "Written Statement of Jennifer DeStefano: Abuses of Artificial Intelligence," June 13, 2023, https://www.judiciary.senate.gov/imo/media/doc/2023-06-13%20PM%20-%20Testimony%20-%20DeStefano.pdf.

"Well, *I'm* completely freaked out," Madison said.

Alma reached across and squeezed her daughter's hand. "I know it's scary, but it's better to know about this stuff so we can make a plan for it."

"What should our safe word be?" She asked.

"I think it should be 'Madison sucks,'" Christopher cracked.

"And for that, *you* get to clear the table," Alma said to him. She set her silverware on her plate and held it toward her son, her eyebrows raised. Alma didn't put up with her kids being unkind to each other.

"I was just kidding," Christopher said sulkily, though he did take the plate and head toward the kitchen.

"I'm happy to pitch in, too." Elizabeth pushed her chair back and picked up her plate. "The sooner we clean up, the sooner we eat cake."

As they were loading the dishwasher and packing up the leftovers, James asked, "Elizabeth, how worried should we be about identity theft? It seems way too easy to steal someone's identity right now."

"Well, one thing I find comforting is to remind myself that even though there are a lot of scammers out there, the cybersecurity industry is huge. There are a lot of smart people out there who are constantly working on safeguards. But you're right to be concerned. Personally, I have identity theft insurance."

"It's pretty wild how many industries have cropped up *because* of the internet and AI."

"Totally agree," Elizabeth said emphatically. "Like with AI, there's a lot of worry about how it's going to replace jobs, but we have no idea how many jobs it's going to create."

"I'd love to pick your brain about that," Alma said. "Everybody at work is talking about AI, and no one really knows what to make of it."

"Pick away. I love talking about AI at work."

"Okay, let me make some coffee. You go relax in the living room."

CHAPTER 3

AI at Work

If you're part of the workforce, you've heard that AI is going to dramatically change the way we work.

In a report by Jobs for the Future (JFF) titled "The AI-Ready Workforce," their findings reflect what you've probably already intuited if you're part of the workforce: change *is* coming, but it doesn't necessarily feel like it's fully here. When JFF's report was published in November 2023, fewer than 10 percent of workers surveyed said they were currently experiencing AI on the job, but 58 percent expect they'll need to learn new AI-related skills. Unfortunately, 88 percent of respondents said they don't trust their employer to support them in understanding AI.[29] These statistics paint a picture of a workforce on the edge of their seats, waiting expectantly to see what comes next and not sure when or how they'll build the skills to keep up.

*****

"It's the unknown that's killing me," Alma said, setting a tray down on the coffee table. Mugs, sugar, creamer, and spoons. She went back to the kitchen to grab the carafe, and the adults sat into it, preparing their coffee to their liking.

---

[29] "The AI-Ready Workforce," Jobs for the Future, November 2023, https://drive.google.com/file/d/13MeCU2dE33CNh2mCgkA422LqD6_malRk/view.

"I work for a retailer that has brick-and-mortar as well as e-commerce. The CEO is itching to cut jobs and replace them with AI, but I honestly think he has no idea what that would entail. He accuses me of being a Luddite when I push back on him." She sat down on the couch and sunk back into the cushions with a sigh, seeming exhausted by the situation. "I'm the Digital Director for our company, and it seems like every week he comes to me with some so-called 'success story'"—here, she rolled her eyes—"of this or that company that laid off X percent of their people because AI can supposedly do their jobs. I worry I'll come into work one day, and he'll have laid off half my team."

"I'm really sorry to hear that." Elizabeth frowned and shook her head. "AI *will* replace some work, but in a lot of cases, it's going to complement and augment the work we humans do."

*****

In "The AI-Ready Workforce," JFF identifies five types of impact, saying that AI will either *replace, displace, complement, augment,* or *elevate* the work of humans. And rather than replacing entire roles, it's more likely that AI tools will change our work at the task or skill level.[30] If there's a task that can more easily be done by a computer than a human—like crunching numbers or repetitive mechanical tasks—then yes, those tasks will likely go to AI. But for things that are more complex, nuanced, or unpredictable, we'll likely use AI to support us in doing those things more quickly and effectively.

It's unlikely that *any* industry will be untouched by AI, and there's too much to go into in this short primer, but in this chapter, we'll touch on four industries you're surely familiar with: retail, healthcare, arts and entertainment, and education.

---

[30] "The AI-Ready Workforce."

How AI Is Impacting Retail

Let's look at Alma's workplace as an example. She works for a retailer that has physical locations as well as an e-commerce website. The work they do includes digital and print marketing, selling products in person and online, and fulfilling orders, which involve warehousing, packing, and delivery. Like a lot of organizations, they're thinking about how AI tools could be incorporated into their business, and one thing they're considering is adding an AI-powered chatbot to their website. In a 2023 survey done by Forbes Advisor, 73 percent of business owners said they're either currently using or planning to use an AI chatbot to support customer service.[31] In fact, AI chatbots already handle 65 percent of communications with customers.[32]

To understand how and why AI chatbots change the way we work, it's helpful to understand a bit about the technology. There's a range of sophistication, but generally speaking, the chatbot pulls information from a specific website—in Alma's case, her company's e-commerce site. If you were to visit the site and type a question into the chatbot, it would use a large language model to keep your intent in mind while it searches the website. Its goal is to answer the question well, given the context, and deliver a relevant answer.

Does the AI chatbot really have the power to replace humans? The short answer is "yes, *and*…" So let's look at an example.

Alma's retail company has a call center. When a customer calls with basic questions about products, pricing, or shipping—anything that could be considered a "frequently asked question"—these are what's known as "tier one" customer service requests because they can be answered by someone without a lot of specialized knowledge. However, as long as those FAQs are addressed in the website content, the AI chatbot can just point the customer to the answer they

---

[31] Katherine Haan, "How Businesses Are Using Artificial Intelligence In 2024," *Forbes Advisor*, April 24, 2023, https://www.forbes.com/advisor/business/software/ai-in-business/.

[32] Jeff Beckman, "120+ Chatbot Statistics for 2024 (Already Mainstream)," *Tech Report*, February 29, 2024, https://techreport.com/statistics/chatbot-statistics/.

need. Inevitably, there will still be plenty of tier-two questions that are more unusual or complex and will require human intervention. This creates a scenario where there are fewer call center workers, and the folks who are there will need to be able to handle those more complicated customer concerns.

In a way, that scenario I just described is, in fact, what some people consider a worst-case scenario with AI, because it does mean fewer people are needed to pick up the phone at the call center. But AI chatbots don't run themselves! At Alma's company, they'd be smart to look at their customer service team and train a few of them to be chatbot administrators. These administrators use their understanding of the business to ongoingly teach and refine the chatbot. They review interaction logs to see what questions customers are asking, how they were answered, and whether the customers found the information helpful. They analyze customer feedback to determine how to improve the chatbot experience. Or they may see instances where the website didn't have the information the customer was looking for, and so they can request that content be created.

And that's just what it takes to administer a chatbot from a customer service perspective. That's the tip of the proverbial iceberg. There's a small army of people needed for strategy, design, software development and testing, AI engineering, security, compliance, and more. So if anyone is saying AI is going to cost us jobs, they're not wrong, but there's no telling how many new jobs will be created as technologies advance and become a bigger part of our day-to-day.

Beyond the Bot: More Ways to Work With AI

Of course, chatbots are just one type of AI tool transforming the way we work in a retail environment. There's seemingly no end to the innovation in progress.

For operations or project managers, you can use an AI webchat to generate spreadsheets, templates, meeting agendas, or reports, which you can then export and edit in Microsoft 365 or Google Workspace. And there are AI tools that can take meeting notes for you and summarize them with varying levels of detail. So, for example, you could create a high-level summary for your executive stakeholder and a more detailed summary for the delivery team.

For marketers and content creators, you can use an AI webchat to do research, come up with ideas for marketing campaigns, or write custom content. There's also a slew of AI image generators like Copilot, ImageFX, and DALL-E, where marketers can create images for use in web content, email marketing, or social media.

Website designers and developers can get in on it, too, using AI tools to design web pages, generate code, and perform testing.

If your organization uses Microsoft 365 or Google Workspace, you can opt in to use their generative AI tools (Copilot and Gemini, respectively) to do all of the above and more—with the major benefit of a closed environment. Meaning, your company can pay for a private instance of the AI tool, which gives access to the enormous pools of data that generative AI tools pull from, but without sending your company data back to that pool. So it's effectively a one-way street that allows businesses to capitalize on what generative AI has to offer without potentially compromising proprietary information.

* * * * *

"This is all much more encouraging than I thought it would be," Alma said. She gave a sheepish smile. "I guess I've been putting my head in the sand a bit."

"You're not alone," Elizabeth reassured her. "There are still people thinking the hype about AI will burn out, and we can all get back to business as usual."

Madison spoke up. "What about me, Aunt Elizabeth? I'm going to nursing school next year. Will I have to learn AI?" She looked cautious but excited by the prospect.

"For sure," Elizabeth said. "We'll always need good people in the medical field—there's really no replacement for the human touch. But AI is already having an incredible impact in healthcare, and you'll get to be a part of it."

TERRI CARBONE

AI in the World of Medicine

AI technology is already revolutionizing healthcare behind the scenes, and you may have already benefited without even knowing.

Every day, surgeons perform procedures using AI-enhanced robots, which means surgeries can be done less invasively and with greater precision. The pharmaceutical industry is harnessing AI's ability to process massive amounts of data very quickly in order to speed up the delivery of new drugs. AI-powered translation tools can improve communication between doctors and patients who speak different languages.

With just those three examples, we can see that AI is already having a profound influence on healthcare by increasing precision, speed, and communication. Yet, Americans are divided on their opinions of the use of AI in healthcare. According to a 2023 survey from Pew, respondents were fairly evenly split between thinking that using AI to diagnose and treat disease would result in outcomes that were better (38 percent), worse (33 percent), or make no difference (27 percent).[33] That's part of my inspiration for writing this book, because I believe that the more we know about AI, the more we can appreciate the good it can do.

Let's take cancer screening as an example. Lung cancer is the second most common cancer to affect both men and women, and the American Cancer Society estimates a quarter million new cases will be diagnosed in 2024 in the US.[34] Unfortunately, due to the lack of symptoms in early-stage lung cancer, most people aren't diagnosed until the cancer has progressed to stage-four metastatic cancer. Because early detection is crucial for better outcomes, doctors and engineers from Massachusetts General Hospital and MIT have devel-

---

[33] Michelle Faverio and Alec Tyson, "What the Data Says about Americans' Views of Artificial Intelligence," *Pew Research Center*, November 21, 2023, https://www.pewresearch.org/short-reads/2023/11/21/what-the-data-says-about-americans-views-of-artificial-intelligence/.

[34] "Key Statistics for Lung Cancer," American Cancer Society, last updated January 29, 2024, https://www.cancer.org/cancer/types/lung-cancer/about/key-statistics.html.

oped an AI-driven solution to aid detection. A human—no matter how skilled and thorough they are—can't evaluate an image to the same microscopic level of detail that can be achieved by a machine. Their system, called Sybil, is an algorithm that can be used to review lung scans and predict whether a person will develop lung cancer. In studies, Sybil was 94 percent accurate.[35]

* * * * *

"I sure wish we'd had this technology when Dad was still alive," James said. The family nodded. For a moment, all were quiet, thinking of their patriarch—Lynn's departed husband—who had passed away from cancer.

"It's nice to think of all the people who'll survive," Madison said, wiping away tears. "It gives me hope."

"Do you think you'll work with cancer patients?" James asked her.

"Maybe," Madison said. "But all this talk of AI is making me think about studying technology instead. If I could help make AI tools like Sybil, I could help thousands of people. Maybe more."

Her dad beamed at her with pride. "I believe it, kiddo."

AI in Arts and Entertainment

"Christopher, what about you?" Elizabeth asked her nephew. "What do you want to do when you grow up?"

"I want to work on movies," he said, eyes gleaming. "Maybe I'll be an actor. Or write screenplays. Or be a director."

This was a surprise to nobody. Christopher is a born artist and spent his toddler years driving his parents crazy, fingerpainting all over the walls, and playing drums on the pots and pans. But his

---

[35] "AI Could Revolutionize Cancer Detection, According to MIT, Mass General Research." *NBC News* YouTube channel, April 11, 2023, YouTube video, https://www.youtube.com/watch?v=3EV6ryG2j7E.

passion really took off in elementary school when he was cast as Jack in "Jack in the Beanstalk." Ever since then, he's had stars in his eyes and big dreams. He even has a poster of the Hollywood sign hanging above his dresser.

"Well, you're only fifteen, so things are going to change a lot between now and then," Elizabeth said. "But I can at least tell you about some of the ways AI is affecting the industry today."

*****

We've already talked about generative AI tools like webchats, which can be incredibly useful for research and writing, and we've touched briefly on static image generators, which allow you to whip up unique images with just a written description. There are also video generators like Sora (from OpenAI, makers of ChatGPT), which give you the power to create a video just by describing it in words. There are also AI tools that provide subtitles or voiceover, write scripts, edit videos, create animations, and clone people's voices and likenesses to create computer-generated actors.

The upside of these tools is that, whether or not you consider yourself an artist or creator, or you have a lot of technical savvy, it's fun to play, explore, and create unique content without needing a whole team of technical experts. Even if you're not in arts and entertainment, you might find ways to play with these technologies. Maybe you've toyed with the idea of starting a YouTube channel on a topic you're passionate about, but you don't know anything about video production. There are platforms out there that let you upload a script and then automatically generate a video with relevant imagery, subtitles, and voiceover. Or maybe you're in charge of your church newsletter and wish you could add some visual interest. You could easily use generative AI to create eye-catching illustrations that are relevant to your newsletter topic. Or perhaps you're an aspiring songwriter. If so, you could upload your lyrics to an AI tool, which then lets you add instruments and experiment with genre, mood, and tempo.

However, as you can probably imagine, tools like these have created a big shake-up in the arts and entertainment industries. There are concerns about job displacement, similar to what we talked about with Alma's retail company, but with the addition of hot debates about content ownership.

Copyright Conflicts with Generative AI

We've talked about "training data," which are databases of content that AI tools pull from in order to generate the writing, imagery, or video that fulfills your prompt. Training data is scraped from all over the internet—websites, social media, and books—and the original creators are not compensated or even notified that their work has been harvested. This gigantic pool of scraped data is what gets synthesized into seemingly new content when you type in your prompt. The AI developers are, of course, making money with these tools and services, none of which would be possible without the plethora of content they've taken from unwitting creators.

As you might expect, lawsuits cropped up right away from content creators claiming that AI developers have infringed on their copyright, and I'm sure there will be others by the time this book makes its way into your hands. One of the questions at the center of the debate is whether AI developers are within the bounds of "fair use" laws. In the US, there are laws governing the "fair use" of copyrighted material, and one of the tenets of fair use is that small amounts of copyrighted material can be used without permission.[36] One of the contested ideas is whether the bits and pieces of the harvested data are substantial enough to be "owned" by anyone. For example, if an image generator is pulling together pixels, lines, shapes, and colors, it could be argued that those fall within the bounds of fair use, even though, in the grander sense, generative AI tools would not exist without the copyrighted content they've scraped from the internet.

---

[36] "US Copyright Office Fair Use Index," *US Copyright Office*, last updated November 2023, https://www.copyright.gov/fair-use/.

These are new issues for lawmakers and courts, and it'll take some time for legal precedents to take shape. But in the meantime, corporations and creators are taking their own actions.

Take Adobe, for example. Since the 1980s, they've been developing software to enable creativity, including products for visual design, publishing, photo editing, and video production. (Even if you've never used their products, you've surely heard of their most famous one: Photoshop.) Adobe's AI image generator is called Firefly, and—whether it's out of genuine corporate virtue or a pragmatic desire to *not* infuriate their customers—Adobe has been careful to develop Firefly in an ethical, transparent way that respects the role of the creator. A portion of Firefly's training data comes from Adobe's own stock image shop; it's an e-commerce marketplace where photographers, illustrators, and videographers can sell licenses for the use of their work. Adobe has enabled an option for these sellers to tag their work as "do not train," which will prevent that work from being used as training data for Firefly. What's more, Adobe is striving to make this option an industry standard.[37]

While it's understandable that creators are worried about the unlicensed use of their work, it's heartening to know that there are companies like Adobe that are proactively taking a socially conscious approach to artificial intelligence, even before definitive legislation forces their hand. And Adobe is not alone. The Biden-Harris Administration has gathered voluntary commitments from leading technology companies—including Adobe, Google, Microsoft,

---

[37] Dana Rao, "Building Safe, Secure, and Trustworthy AI: Adobe's Commitments to Our Customers and Community," *Adobe blog*, September 12, 2023, https://blog.adobe.com/en/publish/2023/09/12/adobes-ai-commitments-to-customers-and-community.

IBM, Amazon, and others—to develop AI technologies that are safe, secure, and trustworthy.[38,39]

AI at Schools

"This all makes me really curious about how we could be using AI at school," James said.

"It does?" Elizabeth's eyes lit up.

"Maybe I should start asking around and see what the other teachers are up to. Maybe we could talk to the principal, form a committee, or something. There's got to be a ton of opportunity. I just have no idea what it is."

Elizabeth was impressed. She knew James wasn't *opposed* to AI, but it would be very cool if her brother actually became an advocate for it. Too many people were in a reactive position, waiting to see how AI would affect them, when she knew we could all be doing so much more to proactively empower ourselves and find ways to use these tools to make our lives easier.

"What are your biggest pain points as a teacher?" Elizabeth asked.

"Geez, where to begin?" James blew out a sigh and ran a hand through his hair. "Well, off the top of my head, I'd say none of us teachers feel like there's enough time in the day to do everything we need to do." He started ticking off on his fingers. "Lesson planning,

---

[38] US White House, "Fact Sheet: Biden-Harris Administration Secures Voluntary Commitments from Leading Artificial Intelligence Companies to Manage the Risks Posed by AI," press release, July 21, 2023, https://www.whitehouse.gov/briefing-room/statements-releases/2023/07/21/fact-sheet-biden-harris-administration-secures-voluntary-commitments-from-leading-artificial-intelligence-companies-to-manage-the-risk s-posed-by-ai/.

[39] US White House, "Fact Sheet: Biden-Harris Administration Secures Voluntary Commitments from Eight Additional Artificial Intelligence Companies to Manage the Risks Posed by AI," press release, September 12, 2023, https://www.whitehouse.gov/briefing-room/statements-releases/2023/09/12/fact-sheet-biden-harris-admini stration-secures-voluntary-commitments-from-eight-additional-artificial-intelligence-companies-to-manage-the-risks-posed-by-ai/.

teaching classes, grading tests and homework, tutoring the students who need extra help, communicating with the parents. My to-do list is endless."

* * * * *

An overwhelming to-do list is a hallmark of many jobs these days, but teachers deserve special attention given the special role they play in society. So much is expected of teachers. They nurture our children at pivotal points in their development and often do so from inside a pressure cooker of competing expectations from administrators, parents, and government regulations. It's a rewarding but taxing profession, and our teachers deserve all the help they can get.

We've already seen how AI tools can help automate routine tasks or quickly generate new content. By this point in the book, you probably know more about AI than the average person, and so I'm sure you can already guess how AI tools can be applied to education, too. A busy teacher could gain a lot of breathing room in their day by using an AI webchat to create a lesson plan, a grading rubric, or draft an email to parents—and even translate the email into different languages if that's useful. A teacher could use an AI image generator to add attention-grabbing visuals to a presentation or use an AI video service to turn a written lesson plan into a video with visuals, subtitles, and voiceover.

Of course, there are a slew of products on the market that are tailored to the unique needs of teachers and students. One such product is Diffit, an AI-powered website that lets educators adapt materials to meet different grade levels. Take James, for example. He teaches both Standard and Honors English classes to tenth graders and every year, he teaches *The Great Gatsby*. James is always on the lookout for new and interesting resources to keep things fresh. So let's say he goes to YouTube and finds a great lecture in the book, but the lecture is geared toward college students. He could upload the video to Diffit just by copying and pasting the YouTube link, and Diffit would generate lesson-planning materials that are appropriate to the tenth-grade level. This could include a summary of the video, key

AI MADE EASY

takeaways, vocabulary words, discussion questions, slideshow presentations, worksheets, and quizzes. And if he wants to create some extra challenge for his honors group, he could adjust the grade level to, say, twelfth grade. Now James has *two* complete sets of materials and activities, and it took him less than five minutes.[40]

* * * * *

James's jaw was dropped. "That sounds amazing. I need to try that."

"Right?! There are a lot of incredibly cool tools out there," Elizabeth said. "That's why I love telling people about AI. There's literally something for everybody."

"It would save so much time, and it'd give me the freedom to experiment and try new things. Sometimes I lean on the tried-and-true stuff I've done a dozen times before just because I don't have time to sit down and come up with something different." He looked thrilled by the possibilities.

"Tell me more," Elizabeth said. "What other pain points do you and your colleagues experience?"

"Well..." James looked hesitant. "I hate to bring down the mood, but honestly, a lot of us are really scared about a school shooting." He didn't like to bring up the topic, especially in front of Lynn. He knew his mom worried about him.

As if reading her son's mind, Lynn said, "I always thought teaching was a safe career. But it seems like there's a new shooting just about every week."

"More like every *day*, unfortunately," James corrected her. "There were nearly three hundred fifty school shootings in the US in 2023."[41]

They were left speechless for a moment, and no one was sure how to respond to such a tragic fact.

---

[40] Diffit, accessed April 24, 2024, https://web.diffit.me/.
[41] Christopher Wolf, "School Shootings by State," *US News and World Report*, January 5, 2024, https://www.usnews.com/news/best-states/articles/states-with-the-most-school-shootings.

Finally, Lynn said woefully, "Can AI save us from *that*?"

"That's going to take a much grander solution, unfortunately, but there are ways AI can help," Elizabeth said.

* * * * *

In the United States, the ever-growing epidemic of school shootings is a senseless tragedy that is largely avoidable, but we can't seem to gain a consensus on how to keep our kids and educators safe. While governments and law enforcement dither, it's been left to schools to develop "active shooter" protocols and live under a cloud of unease.

Fortunately, there are some innovative AI developers that are stepping up to address this urgent problem. One of these is ZeroEyes, which uses AI image recognition to identify firearms. Using cameras installed in and around schools, ZeroEyes monitors the video feed, and if the AI algorithm identifies a gun, a ZeroEyes security professional is alerted within seconds. This person reviews the image in question, and if they see that it is, in fact, a gun, he or she then takes the next appropriate steps to alert onsite security and local law enforcement.[42]

If this technology sounds familiar, that's because it is. Back in chapter one, we talked about smart doorbells like Nest, which monitors a video feed at your front door and notifies you when it detects a person or package. The AI algorithm in a product like ZeroEyes performs a fundamentally similar function—it compares the images in front of it with the images in a stored set of training data. However, the difference is in the training data, as you might expect. A smart doorbell is trained on images related to the typical kinds of interactions you might have at your front door, while ZeroEyes is trained on an image set of firearms. As you become more and more aware of the AI around you, you'll see how similar technologies are employed for a multitude of uses.

---

[42] "ZeroEyes Gun Detection Technology," ZeroEyes, accessed April 23, 2024, https://zeroeyes.com/technology/.

Of course, no single tool will solve the multifaceted problem of gun violence in our schools, but AI firearm detection could certainly be part of a larger program to prevent, detect, and respond to these tragic events.

*****

James shook his head. "I'm kind of in awe. I actually had no idea AI could do something like prevent a school shooting."

"I think it's sad that we even *need* this kind of technology," Lynn sniffed.

"I agree, Mom," Elizabeth said. "But I try to focus on the positives, and feel grateful that they exist."

"True," Lynn said. "It's encouraging to know there are people out there trying to make a difference."

"Hey, Aunt Elizabeth," Madison broke in, a puzzled look on her face. "What I don't get is why so many people are worried about AI? From what you've told us, it sounds like a good thing."

Elizabeth sighed, not quite sure where to begin with the complexity of it all. Fortunately, she was saved by her mom saying, "Before we get into all that, I think it's time for birthday cake." "And ice cream!" Christopher added.

"And ice cream," Lynn confirmed, ruffling his hair on her way to the dining room.

CHAPTER 4

Responsible AI

After a delightfully off-key rendition of "Happy Birthday," the family sat once again around the dining room table, this time with plates of chocolate cake topped with scoops of ice cream. They dug in, momentarily silent, while they enjoyed Lynn's famous cake, which was always a crowd-pleaser.

Finally, Elizabeth said, "Back to your question, Madison. You asked why some people are worried about AI."

"Yeah," Madison said. "I don't get it. It's really cool technology, and it sounds like it's being used to save lives. Is it just because AI is new?"

"I'm sure that's part of it," Elizabeth said. "AI is bringing up a lot of change, and change can be stressful to navigate. And while it's true that AI is being put to some very good uses, it's more complicated than that…"

The Unsettled State of AI Technologies

As you now know, we're already swimming in AI. Even though, for many of us, our awareness of AI began with the explosion of tools like AI webchats and image generators, AI technology has been a part of our everyday lives in ways we hardly think twice about, like with smartwatches or car safety systems. If you've gotten a medical diagnosis or had a surgical procedure in the past few years, AI might have been a silent but crucial member of your medical team.

Though people can be put off by the "artificial" aspect of artificial intelligence, these technologies are a testament to *human* intelligence. They've been developed by smart, inventive folks worldwide, and as you can see from just the dozen or so applications we've talked about in this book, they're coming up with some ingenious ways to help us save time, be more creative, and solve some very pressing problems.

However, in some ways, AI is the Wild West. New developments are happening daily, and there's very little oversight or industry regulation, which can stoke anxieties about unforeseen consequences. These powerful new tools have compounded the preexisting problems that have stemmed from the lack of data privacy and the shady dealings of data brokers. As quickly as AI developers create new technologies, scammers are exploiting them to find new ways to defraud people, while, on the other hand, cybersecurity professionals hustle to anticipate, prevent, and respond to new threats. Incredible change is happening at an incredible pace, and the consequences are unfolding as we speak. It's normal to feel unsettled by the frenzy, even when you can see the many positives in the technology.

AI's Biggest Weak Spots

With AI's growing ubiquity, it has the potential to impact our lives in very real ways, and given AI's weak spots, those impacts aren't always for the better. More and more, companies are leaning on AI algorithms to make decisions about hiring, home and auto loans, credit card approvals and credit limits, apartment rentals, and more. Law enforcement is using algorithms to identify criminal suspects. These are all areas where, historically, entrenched biases have prevented all Americans from having equal access and protection.

Algorithms aren't inherently the problem. As we covered in Chapter one, an algorithm is a set of rules or processes that a system follows. Data goes into a system, is processed through a set of rules, and a result comes out the other side. However, though the algorithm itself is neutral, it can produce biased outcomes depending on the quality of its training data. And in cases where AI is trained to use historical data to make decisions or predictions, it can perpetuate outdated prejudices based on characteristics like race, gender, sexual orientation, or disability status.

For example, anyone seeking a job these days has likely faced an applicant tracking system (ATS). They're the scourge of many job seekers, as they use algorithms to automatically screen applicants with no transparency or explanation as to what criteria they're using. Currently, there are no legal requirements for companies to disclose whether they're even using AI to make hiring decisions.[43] Job seekers are frustrated with a system that feels broken and unfair, and they're not wrong to be skeptical. In a 2024 article from ACLU titled "Busting Bias in AI," the authors share a couple of pertinent examples of AI bias: Between 2014 and 2017, Amazon's hiring algorithm reportedly ranked resumes lower if they contained the word "women." And in a different example, an AI resume screener ranked applicants higher if they played lacrosse in high school or their name was Jared.[44] Given how commonplace these ATS are, you can see how these biases would favor white, able-bodied men over other qualified job seekers.

But There's Good News

Given that AI is the greatest technological revolution since the advent of the internet, it's natural to compare the two phenomena. When the internet arrived, we didn't know what to make of it—and we couldn't even Google it yet! For a lot of people, adapting to the internet requires a fairly steep learning curve. Some of us were reluctant to adopt an unproven technology, worried about our privacy,

---

[43] Wudan Yan, "Busting Bias in AI," *ACLU Magazine*, American Civil Liberties Union, Spring 2024, 18–23, https://www.aclu.org/wp-content/uploads/2024/02/ACLU_SPRING24_Spreads-compressed_0224.pdf.

[44] Yan, "Busting Bias in AI."

put off by the costs, or just didn't see its usefulness in our own lives. It's the same set of concerns people now have about AI, but the difference is this: we're *all* more tech-savvy, as individuals and as a society. Anything you want to know about AI, you can find in articles, videos, and classes created by passionate technologists and educators—like our fictional friend Elizabeth—who relish the chance to share their knowledge.

On a more "macro" scale, governments, fair-minded corporations, and nonprofits are paying attention. They're well aware of the current problems with AI technologies, and each, in their own way, is trying to help. In October 2023, the US White House issued an executive order on the "safe, secure, and trustworthy development and use of artificial intelligence" to guide the country in harnessing AI's potential while mitigating its risks.[45] And it isn't just a feel-good idea, either; the Biden-Harris Administration is backing up their words with action. In March 2024, Vice President Harris announced that the White House Office of Management and Budget had issued a set of policies aimed at federal agencies. Without getting into the weeds, here's a concrete example (from a White House fact sheet) of the kinds of safeguards enshrined in these policies: "When at the airport, travelers will continue to have the ability to opt out from the use of TSA facial recognition without any delay or losing their place in line."[46] That's just one small example, of course, but I hope it's heartening to know our government is proactively addressing the real-world implications of AI adoption.

---

[45] US White House, "Executive Order on the Safe, Secure, and Trustworthy Development and Use of Artificial Intelligence," press release, October 30, 2023, https://www.whitehouse.gov/briefing-room/presidential-actions/2023/10/30/executive-order-on-the-safe-se cure-and-trustworthy-development-and-use-of-artificial-intelligence/.

[46] US White House, "Fact Sheet: Vice President Harris Announces OMB Policy to Advance Governance, Innovation, and Risk Management in Federal Agencies' Use of Artificial Intelligence," press release, March 28, 2024, https://www.whitehouse.gov/briefing-room/statements-releases/2024/03/28/fact-sheet-vice-president-harris-announces-omb-policy-to-advance-governance-innovation-and-risk-management-in-federal-agencies-use-of-artificial-intelligence/.

As for corporations, we know they're primarily motivated by profits. I don't blame you if you're thinking corporations will take advantage of every inch of legally available wiggle room to harvest your data and market their products to you—using AI to supercharge those efforts. However, corporations and the people who populate them aren't immune to the risks of AI. Early in 2024, news broke about a finance clerk for a multinational company who was manipulated into sending $25 million to a group of scammers. The criminals invited the clerk to a video conference and used deepfake technology to mimic an entire group of the company's top executives, including the Chief Financial Officer, who "authorized" the release of funds.[47] So both personally and professionally, corporate leaders are motivated to find ways to develop and use AI responsibly.

Fortunately, while our government moves slowly, corporations are more nimble, and some of the leading technology companies are making efforts to protect the public good. We've already talked about Adobe and their efforts to mainstream the option for content creators to opt out of having their work used to train AI algorithms. Another example is Google. Given today's epidemic of misinformation, Google has programmed its AI webchat, Gemini, to prevent it from answering any questions related to a country's upcoming election.[48] A third example is the Coalition for Content Provenance and Authenticity (C2PA), which is one of many corporate coalitions in which industry leaders are voluntarily banding together to create reasonable standards. In the case of C2PA, they've developed technology that identifies the origin of a digital media file, like a photo or video, and creates a secure log of all edits that are made to the file. Technology like this allows reputable news outlets to ver-

---

[47] Drew Todd, "Hong Kong Clerk Defrauded of $25 Million in Sophisticated Deepfake Scam," *Secure World*, February 13, 2024, https://www.secureworld.io/industry-news/hong-kong-deepfake-cybercrime.

[48] Jagmeet Singh, "Google Won't Let You Use Its Gemini AI to Answer Questions about an Upcoming Election in Your Country," *Tech Crunch*, March 12, 2024, https://techcrunch.com/2024/03/12/google-gemini-election-related-queries/.

ify the authenticity of their images and alerts viewers if an image is doctored.[49]

And, of course, there are not-for-profit groups dedicated to research, education, and equity. As corporations develop the technologies and governments develop the laws, non-profits are watching out for the people. Researchers, AI ethicists, technologists, and justice advocates are pushing corporations and governments to develop and use AI in accordance with our democratic ideals and to represent the interests of people who have been historically marginalized. One not-for-profit group is the Algorithmic Justice League, which was founded by Dr. Joy Buolamwini, an accomplished computer scientist and activist. While at MIT, her project titled *Gender Shades* found that facial recognition software routinely failed to accurately identify the faces of darker-skinned women. Her paper on the topic prompted Microsoft and IBM to improve their software.[50,51] With the Algorithmic Justice League, Buolamwini and her colleagues are working to identify and eliminate harm caused by AI.

Governments, corporations, and not-for-profits have different agendas, of course, but this creates a productive environment of checks and balances that will, ideally, result in the ongoing development of technologies that are financially sustainable, fair for *all* people, and reflect our civic ideals.

Responsible AI is in *Your* Hands

While on the macro level, you and I have a limited ability to influence lawmakers and corporations, on the micro level, we have an *unlimited* ability to influence ourselves. AI is here to stay, and your choice is whether to engage with it consciously or unconsciously. There is no opting out. AI can happen to you, or it can happen *with*

---

[49] Coalition for Content Provenance and Authenticity, accessed April 28, 2024, https://c2pa.org/.
[50] "Joy Buolamwini," *Wikipedia*, last updated May 8, 2924, accessed May 13, 2024,
[51] https://en.wikipedia.org/wiki/Joy_Buolamwini.

you. The choice is yours. My hope is that, after reading *AI Made Easy*, you're feeling wiser and more excited about AI than you were at the outset, and that this is only the start of your lifelong learning on the topic. If you stay attuned to technological changes, experiment with new tools as they arise, and think critically about them, you can tap into the benefits of AI—personally and professionally—and avoid a lot of the downsides. Remember: AI is just a tool, and, like all tools, it can be used for good or for bad. I encourage you to be smart, not fearful.

As we all go forward in this new world, it's helpful to remind ourselves to keep a healthy perspective on technology. Tools will come, go, and evolve. But the simple joys of being a human remain like taking kids to the park or helping them with their homework, attending church, or volunteering to help people in your community. Treasure your friends, your family, and the Lord God. There is no technology that replaces human fellowship, trust, laughter, and love.

* * * * *

The family gathered in the front hallway to say a reluctant goodbye to Elizabeth. "I love spending time with you guys," she said, shrugging herself into her jacket. "I wish I didn't have to go."

"Don't forget your leftover birthday cake," Lynn said.

Elizabeth squeezed her mom tightly. "Thanks, Mom. I love you."

"Aunt Elizabeth, if I have more questions about AI, can I text you?" Madison asked.

"Of course!"

"Me, too?" James asked. "I think I'm going to need your help once I start this conversation at school."

"And I should probably have you talk to some of my friends from church," Lynn added. "I know *I* feel better about all this AI stuff after talking to you. I'm sure they would too."

Elizabeth was thrilled. She could hardly believe her family's turnaround—from AI skeptics to AI evangelists, all in the course of one meal!

"I would absolutely love to help," she said sincerely. "Any time."

ABOUT THE AUTHOR

As someone who has had a long career in the technology industry, I've helped a lot of people adapt to new advancements over the years. I've worked as a programmer and project manager, and I've led technical teams at the director level. In 2019, I completed an MIT certificate in Artificial Intelligence: Implications for Business Strategy and began my journey as an AI strategist and transformation guide for companies. My goal is to help individuals and organizations understand how they can benefit from and successfully adopt AI. My philosophy is that AI is a tool, just like the internet is a tool, and it can be used for good or for evil. But if you get proficient with AI, you can use it to bring great benefits to many people.

Printed in the USA
CPSIA information can be obtained
at www.ICGtesting.com
CBHW022010080824
12906CB00043B/588